GOING HOME

GOING HOME

CAROLINE TOLOFF

GOING HOME

iUniverse books may be ordered through booksellers or by contacting:

iUniverse
1663 Liberty Drive
Bloomington, IN 47403
www.iuniverse.com
1-800-Authors (1-800-288-4677)

Because of the dynamic nature of the Internet, any web addresses or links contained in this book may have changed since publication and may no longer be valid. The views expressed in this work are solely those of the author and do not necessarily reflect the views of the publisher, and the publisher hereby disclaims any responsibility for them.

Any people depicted in stock imagery provided by Thinkstock are models, and such images are being used for illustrative purposes only.
Certain stock imagery © Thinkstock.

ISBN: 978-1-4917-8048-0 (sc)
ISBN: 978-1-4917-8049-7 (e)

Print information available on the last page.

iUniverse rev. date: 11/23/2015

Contents

DEDICATION

This book is dedicated to my children, Marilyn, Terri, Toni, and Peter, as well as my six grandchildren and five great grandchildren. You all have a very special place in my life story.

Acknowledgement

I would like to express appreciation to Morris Publishing for seeing me through my first book project. I would also like to acknowledge my granddaughter, Terri Draper, for her patience and perseverance with the editing process.

PROLOGUE

The date is May, 2014. I'm sitting and gazing at my twelve-year-old granddaughter. Her name is Alexandria, we call her Allie. Summer vacation is about to begin and she can hardly wait. In anticipation, she's climbing, jumping, and running just thinking about it. As I watch her antics, my mind begins to spin the years away, 72 years back to May 1942. I was a twelve-year-old student also anxiously awaiting summer vacation. Little did I know summer plans were being laid out for me by my mom and a cousin in Seldovia named Annie. Surely they wouldn't send me away for three months. I can baby-sit weekends in Seward. Doesn't the Halverson family already have ten kids? They can't be serious and I won't worry about it now. But I'm getting ahead of my story so I'll give you some family history first.

CHAPTER 1

My father, Charles George Curtis, was bon in Bath, England. He served throughout World War I as a wireless radio operator in the British Navy. My father received gun shot wounds in both legs that remained with him until his death. Following the War, he entered commercial work in the same line. He began in 1919 when he went aboard the S.S. Jefferson of the Alaska Steamship Co. as a wireless operator. He also served on the S.S. Victoria, Nizino, and Old Office of Indian Affair ships S.S. Starr and S.S. Boxer. It is said that while serving as Chief Radio Operator of the S.S. Starr, he and First Officer Roy Wheeler installed a broadcast station on the ship and they surprised the town of Seward as they played the harmonica for their first broadcast.

My father and crew on the 4th Avenue dock in Seward
in the early 1920's. He is second from the left.

My mother, Catherine Anderson, was born in Unalaska, AK to parents Andrew Anderson of Norway and Mary of Aleut/ Norwegian descent. My mother lost her parents and younger siblings in the flu pandemic of 1918-1919. Three girls and three boys survived, Andrew, Bill, Paul (Boots), Vera, Mary, and Catherine. The three youngest were placed in the Jesse Lee Home, Bill, Paul, and Catherine. Vera was sent to Chemawa Indian School in Oregon. Andrew and Mary were almost adults at the time.

It is believed my mother was sixteen years old when she left the orphanage and met my father. They married on May 17, 1925 in Unalaska. They moved to Seattle shortly after the marriage, although my dad continued to sail parts of the Aleutian Islands. My brother, Charles Fredrick Curtis, was born in the Swedish Hospital in Seattle on February 6, 1927.

My parents, Charles and Catherine Curtis in Unalaska, 1925

My family moved to Seward in 1928. They moved to the radio station in the early 30's, where my father was the caretaker and continued to broadcast to the ships. He also worked on the freight docks. The radio station was once the hub of Naval radio communication in the 1920's and 30's. It was closed in 1923 due to lack of funds. The forty acre facility sat on the area North of Resurrection Bay and included an operating station, dormitory for six men, quarters for four families, and a concrete power house. It was re-opened in 1926 and taken over by the signal corps. The grounds also included a tennis court and golf course.

After my parents left Seattle, my family had increased to six children between 1928 and 1936 – Charlotte Louise, 1928, Caroline Alice, 1929 Claude George, 1930 (deceased 1935), Claudette, 1936, and Christian Carol, 1938.

From left, Charlie Curtis Jr., Charlotte Curtis, Caroline
Curtis, and Claude Curtis. This photo was taken at the
radio station when I was about three years old.

My family was the only occupants at the radio station other
than Charlie Christianson who lived alone in a little log cabin.
It was a lovely place for children. The local dairy farm herded
their cows to graze along the beach. The daisies, irises, lupine,
and fireweed grew in proliferation. As did sweet peas and goose
tongues, an edible salty green blade of grass. After we moved to
town, my dad would take us to the beach to pick the tasty goose
tongues. My sister Charlotte and I would take turns, perched on
a homemade stool with a large pan of cold water, washing each
blade one at a time. Next we would rinse dandelion greens and
swiss chard from the garden. After high tides, which came right
up to the house, we would look for fascinating little sea creatures.
We also had chickens on the property and the sun stayed up until
late evening.

We were allowed to walk to the airport where the bi-planes
would land. The pilots wore real aviator caps and goggles. They

would share their chocolate with us, which I am sure was part of their survival kit.

On April 29, 1934, an out of control grass fire destroyed the entire facility except for the power house, which stood like a sentry over the ruins for 97 years.

Radio station, Seward AK, prior to the fire

CHAPTER 2

My parents maintained a close relationship with the Jesse Lee Home in Unalaska, as well as the new location in Seward. After we lost our home, we were offered a place to stay at the new Jesse Lee Home. It was a place for us four children to stay until our parents were able to settle in town. The Jesse Lee Home had a huge garden that was maintained by the older boys. The Home also had goats, pigs, and cows. I would say they were pretty self-sustaining! I loved the touch of class at the dinner table when I saw cloth napkins complete with napkin rings.

We were very young and we missed our parents, but the Home was a place of love and kindness and discipline, which we were used to. I think we stayed there about six weeks. Our parents bought a house on First Avenue and we moved home. It was not long before my dad had a large vegetable garden growing at our new home, along with raspberries and rhubarb. He also had a beautiful rock flower garden.

Whenever we had a "shocker" earthquake, dad would shoo us all out the door and start grabbing his many canary bird cages off their hooks from the sun porch. He said they were German Warblers.

My dad began doing radio and electrical repairs at our home. He would be working on several at one time, some to be rebuilt. It was not unusual to see skeletal radios waiting for him to add wires and tubes and turn them into music. There was always a victrola going with the music of Al Jolson, jazz Enrico Caruso, and opera singer Lily Pons, just to name a few from his wonderful collection. I can still hear Rudy Vallee singing, "I'm just a Vagabond Lover."

CHAPTER 3

My father passed away suddenly at the age of 42 on September 1, 1939. He left work on the dock at 6:00 a.m. and he went down the alley from our house to the hospital. They checked him out and sent him home. He passed at 1:00 p.m. We had a lot of support from our friends and neighbors. My dad was a respected man in the community. My mom was fiercely protective of us and she wondered if the welfare people would try to check on us to see if we had enough to eat. She wanted no help and we were warned not to answer the door. My mom took small jobs around town, mostly working as a house-keeper for our neighbors and other people who entertained visitors.

We always had a big Christmas when my dad was here. He did the cooking for Thanksgiving and Christmas. He made miniature mince meat pies, and he also made English food like chutney and tea with milk. He would order our Christmas gifts from the Sears and Roebuck catalog. After he was gone Christmas became a little scarce. But it didn't bother us, we were happy with small things and the kindness of our neighbors.

When I turned 12 years old in the Fall of 1941, I was not really aware that there was a war going on. I heard what happened in Pearl Harbor, but that was a long way across the ocean. We woke up one morning and saw our whole world had changed and would never be the same. It was known that 3,278 enlisted men and 171 officers had come to our town. They were every where, along with their military vehicles. They would all be stationed at Fort Raymond on the edge of town. That was a huge input of people to our little town, and it was a large financial benefit to the city. My mom started doing laundry service for some of the soldiers. They would drop off their laundry and she would wash, iron, and fold it for them to pick up later. We became acquainted with some of the boys, hardly much older than my brother. They were friendly and appeared to be lonely for company and would stay and visit. Sometimes they would bring a bag of doughnuts to share, actually, quite often.

Life was easier for my mom and she could quit worrying about the welfare people. She had a steady income.

CHAPTER 4

My aunt Mary Halverson lived in Seldovia. She had ten children, ages two to 21. Her daughter, my cousin Annie, would visit quite often. She had a two-year-old daughter. When Annie stayed with us, she liked to take me to town with her to shop. She would buy me little surprises.

In the Spring of 1942, Annie and mom discussed the idea of me going to Seldovia at the end of the school year to baby-sit her little girl. I would leave on May 22nd and Annie would see that I got back at the end of August. She would be working in the cannery and I would be paid wages for those three months. I was not included in the conversation.

It didn't come as a complete surprise when on May 22, 1942, while my sister and I were at the movie, a familiar face approached us. Bob King was a friend of my mom and also the Halverson family. He was a deck-hand on the fishing vessel, St. George – the boat that would take me away from my family for eighteen months. He said, "Caroline, you have to come with me. The boat is leaving in 30 minutes."

My sister Charlotte appeared speechless as I walked away. I recognized a bag he carried which held a few personal items of mine. I left the theater and we went to the end of the Fourth Avenue dock in Seward. As we climbed down the ladder, I could hear the *chug-chug* of the engine and the air was heavy with gas fumes.

CHAPTER 5

A lady and a small girl were already there. I learned she was the skipper's wife. They were a family. I looked at Bob as though he was my only friend in the whole world.

As we got under-way, I thought, *I have no idea where I'm going or how long it will take to get there.* I was not happy, I had a toothache, and somebody was eating my doughnuts at home. There was also a large expanse of black water ahead of me.

I tried to settle in but being alone on the water in the dark, I thought about our home and my family. They would be visiting their company and sharing the doughnuts. In retrospect, I think of Allie and how she would feel at the age of twelve and was alone headed to a strange place. I remember I tried to go to sleep and not think of anything, but the fumes and noise made it impossible. Annie was always good to me and I wasn't afraid to meet my aunt and cousins, it was just so far away and such a strange place. I wished it was only going to be for a weekend. That sounded exciting.

Our one stop was Portlock, a ghost-town near Port Chatham and just east of the abandoned town of Chrome. Remains of a mine tunnel, house pilings, and rusted cannery equipment could be seen. A U.S. Post Office was opened in Portlock in 1921. Portlock-Chatham was also the site of a territorial boarding school. After a series of unexplained deaths, the town was suddenly abandoned around 1949, and the Post Office closed in 1950. Now it's a historical site.

We pulled up to Anderson's dock in Seldovia at mid-day. It was a beautiful day and the sun was shining. Two of my cousins met me there. Previously, I had met Margaret when she spent time at the hospital in Seward with a broken leg. The eldest was Teddy who had spent almost all of his youth at the hospital in Seattle as he was treated for tuberculosis of the bone. He would stop in Seward on his way to and from Seattle.

The cousins that met me were friendly and pretty. They pointed out their house which was straight up the hill from the dock. The house consisted of a kitchen, a central room where the older girls slept, the parents' bed room, and a huge upstairs with three large beds. There was an outhouse in the back. The house accommodated twelve people.

We introduced ourselves when we got to the house and they all took turns deciding who I looked like. My aunt was very warm and sweet, but obviously controlled by the older girls. My uncle was not home at the time as he spent winters at the Snug Harbor Cannery as a night watchman. When he did arrive a week later, he just looked at me as if to say, "She doesn't look like she's going to eat too much."

CHAPTER 6

Seldovia was a beautiful little village with a great history. At one time, it was the largest port on the inlet with the only hospital, post office, and three large fish canneries working around the clock. Anyone could find work and hiring started at 14 years old. The hospital was fully staffed and the St. Nicholas Russian Orthodox Church stood like a beacon over the village. My family and many others were part Scandanavian, English, and Aleut. I noticed no racism among them. Seldovia's wooden boardwalk, boat harbor, and businesses built on piling were picturesque. I would return to visit many times in later years.

I constantly thought of the war and being away from home. I knew the Japanese had bombed my mom's place of birth, as well as Adak and Kiska. I had visions of them coming up the coast, although I don't recall seeing much military in town. We did see a young soldier making his rounds at the tank farm daily carrying a rifle. He was friendly and we always stopped and talked to him. He never did leave Alaska, he married and spent his life here. We knew him very well years later. I heard they did have guard shacks at Outside Beach and other places manned by elderly people of the town with rifles.

CHAPTER 7

It wasn't long before I was a part of the family. Babysitting varied between days and nights, depending on the shifts. There was plenty of time for exploring the back country, picking salmon berries, walking the beaches, and romping through grassy hill sides on breezy summer evenings.

My aunt Mary sent me to the dentist for my toothache. Dr. Kirby was a doctor, not a dentist. I talked Marie, who was my age, into going with me. Dr. Kirby said, "hop right up on that table." He grabbed my mouth and pulled the tooth, no deadening needed. As soon as it was out, I jumped up and ran for the door. I saw Marie running as fast as she could way down the famous board walk. Of course I felt much better.

While I was still the new kid in town, I was stopped by Mr. Adam Lipke of the telegraph office. He said he'd give me a quarter if I would deliver a telegram to Mrs. Juanita Anderson, owner of the dock and cannery. She lived in a huge home that looked like a Southern mansion. I took the quarter and headed down the boardwalk until I came to the double gated yard. As I opened the gates I noticed two big german shepherd dogs on the huge veranda. I only took four steps when one dog came flying at me, grabbed my dress, and took it off. Mrs. Anderson came running down the drive way. She threw something around me and said, "We'll just get you a new dress, Dearie." She took me to the nearby shop and she bought me a navy dress with daises on it. My aunt and cousins just stared at me when I got home and didn't have much good to say about Mr. Lipke.

Summer went by quickly and it was almost time for me to count my wages that I was so proud of earning. I sent my mom a letter. I guess I crossed the line when I said I would be glad to be away from here. I know later that my letters were intercepted and read. I was in trouble then, I didn't get paid or sent home.

I finally had to bend to my older cousin's wishes. One wanted me to sit on the hillside with her while she sang. She had a beautiful voice, I couldn't sing. Another wanted me to smoke a cigarette with her. It made me dizzy. Another wanted me to help her clean cabins for the many bachelors that lived there. I just did what I was told to do. I had no choice. She collected the money.

Annie did buy me items of clothing and I enrolled in the 7th grade. I loved the school and the teachers, especially the music teacher. I wasn't the babysitter anymore. That meant I had time for myself.

Marie and I knew a couple of bachelors who would let us come to their little cabins and use their kitchens and groceries to cook and bake cookies. They were very nice and decent. The best one was the watchman of a cannery. We could bake, take showers, and stay over night. He taught us how to make Norwegian cookies called fattigmann. Marie and I loved cutting out the diamond-shaped cookies, making a slit on one end, and pulling the tip through. That nice man let us use all the ingredients from the kitchen while we made dozens of cookies.

My aunt cooked a lot of fish and beans, always served with Jersey Crackers – a cracker similar to pilot bread with a Jersey cow stamped on one side. Sometimes she baked bread and made fry bread. She worked very hard with little help. My Aunt Mary would make the traditional dish called Perok – a two crust pie (or a 9 x 13 one crust) using salted salmon from a keg and soaked over night. She would layer fish, rice, onion, and other ingredients to take on different flavors such as cabbage, bacon, and boiled eggs. A 9 x 13 pan is most popular and can be cut in squares. It's very tasty and healthy!

At Easter, she would make Paska, also known as Kulich, which is a classic Easter bread that was another dish introduced by Russians. I remember my Aunt saving the one-pound Hills Brothers coffee tins to bake the bread in. She would pour a lemon glaze over the baked bread and add colored sprinkles on top for a festive holiday look.

Sometimes we had music sessions in the kitchen, Annie played the guitar and Edith had a beautiful voice and we all sang. I felt I belonged there so I didn't think about home too much any more.

CHAPTER 8

Thanksgiving was coming and the nice bachelor down the hill from us invited all 12 of us to that little house for dinner. He served a huge, stuffed, turkey and everything to go with it. We all felt blessed.

Following that holiday, our school concentrated on the Christmas pageant. Our choir consisted of all the seventh grade, eighth grade, and high school girls. It was fun practicing and then the day came when the teacher announced that all the girls would wear a white shirt and black skirt. I dashed off a letter to home again and checked the mail every day to no avail. Everything worked out well when they moved me to one end of the chorus line, wearing my beautiful navy dress with the white daisies. No one seemed affected by it, least of all me. It was still a beautiful evening.

Christmas came and went with little to exchange. We had put up a tree in the center room. My uncle Sig came home from Snug Harbor, got drunk, and fell right through the tree. We just looked at it and went dashing down the hill to the Community Hall with it's huge tree. We all sang songs, received a stocking with candy, an apple, an orange, and a gift. Mine was a book – the classic, "Hans Brinker and the Silver Skates." I loved that story and am sorry it was lost somewhere along the way.

It was a quiet time between Christmas and New Years. I don't remember that my aunt's family celebrated the Russian holidays, but Russian Christmas, January 7th, and Russian New Years, the 14th, were alive and well in Seldovia. Starring begins on Christmas day by making a star of brightly-colored paper, sometime a very elaborate star, attached to the end of a stick so as to twirl it. It could have an icon of nativity in the center. Carolers gathered with church leaders, children following, going from house to house where candy and treats were given. This could go on for several nights, if planned. No matter our faith, we all followed the star.

Winter set in and we were back to school. When we had a big snow fall, we all went sliding on the hills, and when it froze we headed to the lake, cleaned off the snow, and built a big fire. I t was a great time to just gather. I never saw a pair of real skates.

As Spring approached, us girls would gather at the Community Hall and dance. We were great dancers to the polka, Swedish waltz, and the schottishe. Us girls danced with each other every chance we had. Selodiva is noted for their dancing and talent for playing musical instruments. Years later, people asked where I learned to dance. I told them I lived in a Scandanavian village for eighteen months.

I missed seeing the huge freight ship make it's annual call to Seldovia the previous year. It was a sight to see laden down with freight, crew, and produce. We all went to the dock hoping they might give us an apple. I was told that all fresh fruit and vegetables went to the store first, and then to people of prestige. Oh well, I'll just wait and get my apple at Christmas time.

As the bustling began for the cannery season, I would dream of going home. I dreamed how I would surprise my family with how independent I had become, and I could help them at home.

CHAPTER 9

I began as before, taking care of Evelyn. I also developed an occasional pain on my right side. It didn't last long, and then in July I doubled over in agony. I took Evelyn in, left her with the other kids, and went over to the hospital. They put me in bed and I believe it was an ice bag they put on my stomach. It eased the pain and I fell asleep.

When I awoke the next morning I felt better. I thought the staff told me they were contacting my mother. I had a perfect view of Seldovia's boat harbor. As I gazed out the window I saw a float plane land in the harbor. I got up and dressed to leave when the nurse came in and asked where I was going. I said, "My mother sent for me to come to the hospital in Seward." She told me to wait right there and she left. When she came back, she said they had not received word from my mom, but it looked like I could go home.

Three days later, as we were all sound asleep upstairs, I awoke all cramped up. At first I thought it was the blistering summer heat until I felt the stabbing pains. Painfully, I pulled on my clothes, crept out quietly, and made my way to the hospital. They took one look at me, put me in bed, slapped an ether cone to my nose, and removed my appendix. I'm appalled even today that they could perform surgery on a minor without consent. I woke up deathly sick from the ether. The hospital staff was good to me. They found it funny when I didn't eat a piece of chocolate pie for lunch and they would bring it back to me with whipped cream for dinner. I was in bed rest for ten days.

CHAPTER 10

August 1943 approached with no mention of my going home. That's when I was told my mom had sold our house in Seward and moved to Anchorage in the middle of the war. Soon it seemed like too much trouble to think about. I could no longer picture the family as it used to be. My home was gone and now my family too. I loved my mother and would never blame her for anything. She was young and doing the best she could. The whole world was in a turmoil. She knew I was with family and that I was safe.

My mother, Catherine Curtis, near Seward, 1950

Far right, Charlie Curtis on top of Mt. Marathon, Seward, AK, early 1920's

Charlie Curtis with his chow named "Sam Shu," Seward, AK, 1928

Caroline Toloff, Anchorage, AK, 1944

My uncle, Paul "Boots" Anderson, Seward, AK, mid-1970's

Me with Billy Mills, 1980. He won a gold medal for the 10,000 meter run in the 1964 Tokyo Olympics. This was considered one of the greatest Olympic upsets. He was the second Native American to ever win the gold ,and the only American to win gold in this event. As President of the Mt. Marathon Native Association, I was asked to host a gathering for Mr. Mills – a proud moment.

Caroline Toloff (left), American Legion Auxiliary President, presenting Benny Benson with an award in Kodiak in 1968. He designed the Alaska state flag in 1927.

My daughter, Marilyn Sieminski. 1953 (age 4), Cooper Landing (Cooper Creek), AK

CHAPTER 11

I had learned to love Seldovia with it's smell of fish "guerries" and retort steam. Fish "gurries" were wagons used to hold the fish heads and guts while cleaning fish. A retort is a vessel used to process canned fish. After the salmon was canned, the cans were put on racks, and the racks were wheeled into the retort to be steam-cooked. Locals sat on the railings of the board walk and discussed the latest news. I loved the quaint shops and wooden floors that smelled like oil. You could put your purchases on credit until the end of fishing season. I could learn to live here.

I loved going to the old stores with their distinctive smells. They had wooden floors cleaned with bleach and oiled. Each store had it's own warmth, especially the variety store which carried most of their wares by the bulk and a wide variety of candy. If you over did putting your choices in a paper bag, the proprietor would weigh it, look at you, and tell you "This isn't going to ring the till," and let you have it anyway. Seldovia was a wonderful, diverse, mix of Alaska Native and Scandanavian culture. The people were warm and generous.

CHAPTER 12

So I began the 8th grade. My subjects were harder and we took classes with high school students. But, I was a good learner and I loved to write poetry and short stories. My teachers read them all, complimented me, and encouraged me to write more.

Then, one day, the second week of November 1943, I was home for lunch. My uncle Sig always had friends visiting. As I kept quiet and ate my lunch I heard one man tell my uncle that Mr. Sharp was taking his boat to Anchorage that day to stay for the winter. I knew Mr. Sharp owned two boats they called sister ships, one was the Pansy and the other was named Violet. I knew that conversation opened the door for me and that I had to go now or maybe never.

The school was right next door to our house, but I slipped around the back way through town. I climbed down the ladder to see four men drinking coffee in the galley. They must have recognized me from the Halverson family when they asked me what they could do for me. I told them the truth – that my family had moved to Anchorage and I needed a ride to join them. He said, "Come along. We're leaving in one hour." I did notice that this vessel was much longer, warmer, and friendlier than the St. George that had brought me here.

I let them know I would be right back. When I got to the house my aunt was alone. I went upstairs first and put a few things in a paper bag. When I came back downstairs, I told her I was leaving on the Pansy. She appeared to understand.

I think she knew I was leaving as she pressed a piece of paper in my hand and explained, "This is a telephone number in Anchorage. Her name is Nellie. She was in Chemawa with your Aunt Vera Roberts. If you have any problems, call her. She will call your Uncle Bill Anderson, he is in the Army in Anchorage." She carefully told me, "Don't be afraid to ask for help. You'll be alright." I remember I felt very sad leaving her, she had been so nice to me and I loved her. We did keep in touch.

After I left she had a baby girl named Patsy. Later years her husband passed away and she married a man named Mr. Sweeney. He was so nice to her and he made life much easier for her. She came to my home in Seward in the early 70's She was terminally ill and wanted to see me. We had a long visit. She loved my home and family. We had a great dinner of deer chops my husband had gotten while on a hunting trip. I never forgot her.

I was in a hurry to get back to the boat. I hugged my aunt and left. My cousins showed up shortly after I went aboard and were on the dock waving as we pulled away.

Once again, I was on a strange boat going to a new destination, and hoping to find my family in a large city. I was overjoyed just thinking about my mom. But it was also a bittersweet feeling now, as the town of Seldovia and family had become a big part of my youth.

The boat crew made me feel comfortable and when we got into rocky seas they settled me in a bunk. One of the crew got his guitar and played a song to me. They made me some tea and were very kind. One member became a close family friend for many years.

It was terribly rough weather and I tried to ease the nausea by thinking of all the kind people I had met in my eighteen months in Seldovia – the man who had fixed a Thanksgiving dinner for a family of twelve, the kindly cannery watchman who let us bake cookies, my music teacher who thought I looked nice in my navy dress with the daisies. Soon I slept.

CHAPTER 13

It was dark out when we arrived at the dock in Anchorage. The crew and myself were immediately surrounded by military as if we were approaching on a foreign submarine. There were so many guards with rifles and cannons pointed at Cook Inlet. We were escorted away separately. I never saw the crew again.

I was taken to a military shack by two military police for questioning. I told them my story and showed them the telephone number of our family friend, Nellie. They left me alone for what seemed like a long time. I wasn't afraid and it was warm inside. I guess they were checking out the telephone number. They returned and I waited for my uncle Bill. He showed up in uniform and took me away.

He had a car waiting for us and we drove away to a house on 9th and East D Avenue, just about the city limits in 1943. There I was reunited with my mom, Charlotte, and Chris. We were overjoyed, but I did not cry. There were no questions asked so there was no explanations needed. To this day, it has never been mentioned.

From left to right, Charlotte Curtis, Charlie Curtis, Caroline Curtis
Front, Christine Curtis

It was great to be together again. I regaled them for days with stories of Seldovia and family. I sang songs that I learned and danced for them. We were all laughing.

The weather was very cold. The day after I got there, mom asked me if I wanted to walk to town. I don't know whose coat I was wearing but the cold went right through it. We stopped at a bar so my mom could talk to the bartender. He looked at me and asked me if I wanted a drink. I said no thank you. There wasn't really much to see on a gray wintry day. I would check it out when it warmed up.

Caroline Curtis (age 14) and Charlotte Curtis (age 15), Anchorage, 1944

Charlotte and I went up town a couple of times in the evening. The streets were crowded with so many people, a lot of soldiers, and activity. There was a lot of noise and the smell of popcorn and pronto pups smelled delicious. The juke boxes blared music from the open doors of the bars. We enjoyed it all. We were young and the gaiety was contagious.

Chapter 14

My Aunt Vera Roberts lived on 10th Avenue and I spent a lot of time at her cozy place. She had eight kids, the three oldest lived elsewhere and five were still at home. The family lived in Anchorage in the winter to attend school, and would leave in the spring for their homestead on Alexander Creek. My Aunt Vera was so sweet and she had the bluest eyes from her Scandinavian side of the family. I spent a lot of time with them.

When the winter warmed up, I would walk 4th Avenue and check out the places. Each time I came to the Rexal Drug Store I would stare at the "hot roasted peanuts" machine. I had no money but I knew I could find a job. I had to. My sister Charlotte had a job and my mom received an allotment from the Government for my brother's service in the Army. That wasn't much income.

My Uncle Andrew and cousins, Lawrence and Earl Roberts, fished commercially in Cook Inlet. They fished for Emard's cannery so they were able to get Charlotte and me jobs in the cannery too. First we worked a couple of months packing fish in cans. Then they moved us to the can loft and we ended up packing the cans in cases and gluing them. It was a fun summer working days, and if the fish was delivered at night, the bus would pick us all up to go to work. I worked with girls from Anchorage and from Palmer. They had a huge party at the end of the season with food and live music.

After the fishing season was over, I would check out 4th Avenue for another job. I really needed to find work. I needed to buy clothes, a coat, and shoes. There was rent to be paid and groceries to buy.

One day, I walked to the end of 4th Avenue. I checked out the Empress Theater, another must on my list. I crossed the street and saw a sign in the window of the Pioneer Laundry that read *Help Wanted.* I went in and told the man that I wanted a job. He looked at me and asked how old I was, I said sixteen, even though I was really only 14. He told me to be there at nine the next morning.

I was there at nine, and it was a long way to walk from 9th and east D Street. There were four of us girls working the mangles, two feeding the sheets through, and two on the other side folding them. We did sheets and bedding for the hotels. At noon the girls said, "Lunchtime!" and went to the little café next door. I went also but I didn't have any money. They shared with me. I knew if I found work closer to 9th Avenue that I would take it.

I worked at the Pioneer Laundry for a couple of months. My sister was changing jobs also. She got a job at the Snow White Laundry. It was owned by a very respected Japanese family, but the parents had been sent to an internment camp. The business was being managed by a couple. When Charlotte told me about the job, I applied as well. That cut about five blocks off my walk. The manager had hired a man that worked all night washing and dry-cleaning clothes. When we arrived in the morning, we spent all day pressing, folding, packaging, and running the counter and customer service. Charlotte became a first-class presser. I knew that laundry work was not for me but we worked well together and we were good at it. The pay was good too. At last I could buy a nice coat and shoes and other things.

After several months there, my cousin Tom Roberts picked me up to give me a ride home. Remember, there were no paved streets in Anchorage at this time except for 4th Avenue. To get to my house was a long ways to walk on gravel. My cousin Tommy drove a coal truck, delivering coal to homes that they used for heating. Tom Roberts would later become a highway patrol man, now called an Alaska State Trooper. He served the Kenai Peninsula and lived in Seward.

As we drove along, he told me of a place that was looking for help. It was a woman named Maude, and she owned a boarding house on 3rd and C street. That sounded good to me.

CHAPTER 15

I met Maude and she hired me. I was still fifteen and on my fourth job. Maude was a hard working woman. She came to Anchorage in 1944 from Montana where she had a boarding house. Back then, it was hard to find a place to start such a business and find a place to live. She found a suitable vacant building which had been closed down by the police. She went to the City and told them if they'd let her, she would open it and run a decent rooming house. An Anchorage bank backed her and she was in business. She charged a moderate price and made the rules just as she did with me. Her rule to the men was no drinking and no women or else out they go. There was no problem. She said working people are almost always nice people and working men respect a good woman. Maude was tough but she had a big heart too. When a roomer moved his family to Anchorage, she had a good, hot, meal ready for them.

After she laid down the schedule and a few rules, we hit it right off. The house had a large front room with four long dining room tables and chairs, a big kitchen, and her rooms in the back. She also had stairs leading to the top floor. The first thing she told me was not to put one foot on those stairs. She said she had six rooms up there for single men and I was never to go up there. That's when I realized she would care for me.

Caroline Curtis and Maude Luoma, Anchorage, 1944

Maude had a new DeSoto convertible, and we'd go to the cannery together to pick up a big halibut. She would butcher it like she did the meat. Maude made big hearty meals, and I would do the salads and vegetables. I was to work at 9 a.m. and be off at 1 p.m., then come back at 3 p.m. until 7 p.m. She paid me a dollar an hour.

I helped prepare food, do the dishes, and carry the food to the tables. It was always a full house, as many of the boarders were men looking for work and they would later send for their families. Many times later in the future, I would recognize a name of someone from the boarding house. They would later become active members of the Anchorage Chamber of Commerce or City Administration. Many of those men made a home and a place for their families and had obtained a renowned position for themselves.

Maude appeared very stern but she taught me the ethics of a good employee. We became very close friends. Some of her boarders also knew I was just a kid and a hard worker. One offered to pay my fare to Bend, Oregon where his mother was the Editor of the newspaper. He said I could stay with her and learn the business, because I was always writing something. They all watched over me and Maude would advise and approve it. One elderly man paid for my dental work. When Maude would be gone, she'd let me stay in her rooms with the big bathroom and a tub. I really enjoyed that.

Maude operated the boarding house until 1954, and she kept the rooming house until it was damaged by the 1964 earthquake. She retired and left the state of Alaska in 1969 after 29 years. She took care of me as if I were her own. She was my dearest friend and a well respected person by the City of Anchorage.

I had become friends with an older girl who was our summer help. When she was through for the summer, she went to work for the North Pole Bakery on 4th Avenue. She talked me into going there as well. After almost a year and a half, I told Maude I was leaving as soon as she could find someone to replace me. It was a somber goodbye. I took the 7:00 a.m. shift at the North Pole Bakery so I could get off early.

CHAPTER 16

All that Winter I about froze to death getting to work in the cold and dark, but I loved the job. My boss was good to me. Soon I was doing specialty jobs too. He had me making ten to twelve boxed lunches everyday which I delivered to the Alaska Airlines office for their in-state flights. The office was on 4ᵗʰ Avenue.

After I was there for six months, I told Harold I had to quit. When he asked why I explained that a Union agent said we had to join the Hotel and Restaurant Workers Union and that I was too young too join. He said, "Don't worry about it." I don't know what he did, but I became a Charter member. We held our meetings by going down the alley behind the First National Bank and into the back room of the Anchorage Funeral Parlor, which faced 5ᵗʰ Avenue. It was a bare and dusty room. We soon had a table and six wooden gasoline boxes to sit on. I was a proud member of the newly formed Hotel and Restaurant Workers Union.

Sometime after that I received a call from Maude. She explained that she had to go to Montana on a business trip and asked if I would consider coming back for a month. I knew the lady I would work with, she had replaced me when I quit. She was married and had three children. We had become good friends. I spoke to my boss and he okayed it as long as I would come back to the bakery. So I changed jobs again and was happy to help.

Soon I was back at the bakery doing errands for Harold. I did the receipts and banking across the street at the only bank in Anchorage. I also found it was easier to run the orders of bread and buns to the businesses on 4th Avenue, The Anchorage Grill, D & D Café, and other restaurants. I loved running those orders to them and soon I knew every business on 4th Avenue. I loved the recognition and I also enjoyed working the retail at the Bakery where I got to meet new people.

CHAPTER 17

At that time, the population of Anchorage was about 15,000 people. It was easy to meet a lot of people. I knew the dress shops, the "Hat Box," and the people who ran the Empress Theater long before the 4th Avenue Theater was opened. I also knew the nearby Presbyterian church that I attended.

There were fun times too. My cousins, the Roberts, were raised in Anchorage and had a wide circle of friends. We went to Palmer. It took two hours of driving on pot holes. We went to Lake Spenard to swim, leaving a trail of dust all the way, and we never met another car on the road. We rented bikes to ride on a short paved 4th Avenue. I bought a little classic black dress and heels and went dancing at the South Seas Club located on a lower level on 4th Avenue. It had bamboo décor to make you feel like you were in Hawaii. People were dressed to the nines and there was band music every night. I was never questioned when I ordered a Singapore Sling cocktail. I had a nice escort and I would sip my drink all evening like a lady. Bad behavior was not tolerated. I loved dancing to the sound of the big band. All the dancing I learned in Seldovia was done at the South Seas.

In the Summer of 1944, I decided to take a vacation and what better place to go than my Aunt Vera Roberts homestead on the Alexander Creek, home of the famous king salmon. My Uncle Andrew Anderson was a along time commercial fisherman of Cook Inlet and would take me to the homestead.

We left the Emard Cannery in his big open dory, clipping across the waters of Cook Inlet. He did a little socializing on the way when another dory from Tyonek kept siding up to our dory, tossing a brown paper bag back and forth. That fools-play caused him to misjudge the tide and we ended up sitting on a sand bar for six hours waiting for the change in the tide. He slept it off while I was steamed at the whole fiasco.

CHAPTER 18

When we reached Alexander Creek, I was taken in by the beauty of it all. My Aunt's cabin sat on the bank of the creek. There was one family with young kids across the creek and one single elder living in a little cabin. The creek ran 35 miles up where another family lived. They would often over-night at my Aunt's place on their way home. It was such a quiet and tranquil setting. I had two cousins there at the time – Leonard, age 16 and Tootsie, age 13. Leonard joined the Marines during the Korean War. Sadly to say, he was killed while making an amphibious landing.

We spent every day paddling the canoe as far as we could up the creek and we would swim in the silty water. The nights were dark and peaceful

Alexander Creek

My Aunt had lanterns for lights and the house smelled of wonderful food cooking. She boiled potatoes from her garden every night to be fried for breakfast along with her big slab of bacon she would slice. It was a real homesteader's breakfast. All her groceries and staples were brought in by plane.

In the evenings, we would play board games or read by the coal oil lamp. We always had the tea kettle on the wood stove ready to go for a good cup of tea along with a strip of smoked king salmon. I've not yet had king salmon as good as my Aunt Vera's. She knew what wood to use and how long to keep it in the smoker. I think we ate salmon every day that had been prepared in her special way. Her porcupine stew was also very delicious.

My Aunt was a very kind person and tolerated our running in and out of the house on long summer days. It was very difficult to come in early to stay. One night a week we learned to be still and keep quiet. That was the night when she turned on the battery operated radio to listen to "Mukluk Telegraph." Mukluk Telegraph was a radio program that communicated messages of importance, emergencies, and announcements to people in the bush. It also communicated messages of arrivals to be picked up and birth announcements. Those who lived in the bush depended greatly on this program.

It was soon time to return to Anchorage and to my job. It was a hard decision to give up the splendor of the creek, the fresh outdoors activity, the smell of wood burning, and the ambiance of living in the bush. I've been to many foreign places but none can compare to the beauty of Alexander Creek.

CHAPTER 19

I returned to work at the North Pole Bakery and spent more time with my friend Laura. Laura was part Athabascan Indian. She worked in an office at the Army post. I would take the bus out there and we would go to the movies and eat in the cafeteria. I considered applying for a job there also, but I didn't have the qualifications. That made me think about my limited education.

I also had my friend Maurice. I met him at the boarding house. He was in the Army but was allowed to live in town as he took care of all the communications and worked for A.C.S. He stayed at the parsonage of All Saints Episcopal Church with Father Fenn located at the corner of 8th Avenue and F Street. The Church was formed with the City of Anchorage in 1915.

Father Fenn was a well known priest for many years in Anchorage and we spent a lot of evenings listening to his stories. Although I attended the Presbyterian Church, which was Reverend Rolland Armstrong's church. He would later perform my wedding ceremony.

Maurice and I would also play tennis at Delaney Park on the grass. We would take his 22 rifle out to Chester Creek for practice. He was a very nice companion. Anchorage was a fun small town. The military was reduced in size and it wasn't so crowded. I liked living there. But I still thought about going home.

CHAPTER 20

I worked for Harold at the bakery until Christmas, 1946. That's when I explained to him that I was leaving. He suggested we sit down and talk. He was my mentor and an integral part of my youth. He told me it was most unusual for someone my age to be a valuable and trustworthy employee. He asked about my future plans and I told him I would be leaving Anchorage. I told him I felt I had led a somewhat nomadic life for five years. He thought that was funny.

I explained that I wanted to finish my education. And I did do that in time. I finished high school and business school, receiving a degree in accounting that gave me a retirement and health benefits from the State of Alaska Department of Education.

I married when I was seventeen. I had three beautiful daughters and one awesome son. I now have six grandchildren that I am just crazy about, and five great grandchildren who are very dear to me.

My children inspired me to put my story on paper. They think I had an amazing youth. And they are right. I had kind and caring family and friends to watch over me. I had the drive and tenacity to find employment, to help my family financially, and to know the difference between right and wrong.

In February, 1947, I boarded the passenger train at the Alaska Railroad Depot in Anchorage. I was on my way to Seward. I was going home.

The Toloff family (from left) Terri, Marilyn,
Caroline, Jimmy, Peter, and Toni

Made in the USA
Coppell, TX
17 December 2021